RYA Youth Sailing Scheme

Syllabus and Logbook

Name	Huyh

First published 2009
Fifth edition 2025

Published by
The Royal Yachting Association
RYA House, Ensign Way, Hamble,
Southampton SO31 4YA
Tel: 02380 604 100
Web: www.rya.org.uk

We welcome feedback on our publications
at publications@rya.org.uk

You can check content updates for
RYA publications at
www.rya.org.uk/go/bookschangelog

Cover design: Doug Bishenden
Cover photos: Paul Wyeth/pwpictures.com,
Sweet Bay Photography, Mark Radford/RYA
Design and typesetting: Doug Bishenden
Photo credits: Paul Wyeth/pwpictures.com,
Sweet Bay Photography, Mark Radford/RYA,
Tim Hampton, Nic Wymer

Printed in the UK

© 2025 Royal Yachting Association
RYA Order Code: G11
ISBN: 978-1-910017562

Contents

Introduction

The RYA Youth Sailing Scheme provides an enjoyable and progressive way to learn to sail. Each certificated course provides an opportunity to recognise your achievements.

Your instructor will sign off each skill as you complete it. Once completed, an RYA certificate will be issued, showing your significant achievement. Your certificate can be of use in contributing to other areas of your study, activities, or The Duke of Edinburgh's Award Scheme. You can also use the skills you are learning towards your PE GCSE, with sailing included on the PE Activity List.

The RYA Youth Sailing Scheme is usually completed in small dinghies suitable for your size.

However, it can also be completed in keelboats and multihulls with some changes to the syllabus and course, e.g. no capsize drill in keelboats.

You can learn to sail well very quickly, provided the equipment is right for you and the challenge suitable. There is provision for guidance and help within the RYA Youth Sailing Scheme, depending on the conditions and what you have to do. In general, you may receive physical help with any part of the syllabus when more strength is required, e.g. on a steep and slippery slipway.

Make sure you can perform all the skills in one course before tackling the next one; otherwise you may waste time relearning skills, or even fail to complete all of the new course.

In this logbook 'With instruction' means 'Can perform the task with a briefing for the conditions, and physical assistance if necessary'.

Courses in the RYA Youth Sailing Scheme are of a minimum length of 16 hours, two days or an equivalent series of sessions. Sailing is a sport that gets better with practice, and you should try to sail between courses whenever possible. Practice makes perfect!

Sailors who are unable to complete parts of the syllabus due to a disability may still receive a certificate, endorsed as necessary, e.g. 'Needs assistance with capsize drill'.

Championship Racing

Regional Racing

Club Racing

First Flights Foiling

Seamanship Skills

Day Sailing

Sailing with Spinnakers

Start Racing

Performance Sailing

Advanced Modules

Stage 4

Stage 3

Stage 2

Stage 1

Following completion of Stage 4, you can further develop your skills through the six Advanced Modules. You may choose any module according to the area of sailing that interests you. Start Racing, Day Sailing, Seamanship Skills or Performance Sailing… the choice is yours! Details of these modules are also available in RYA publication C4, the RYA National Sailing Scheme Syllabus & Logbook.

You can choose either logbook to continue to record your progress. Additionally, there are further race-training courses available to help you improve your performance at club-racing level.

Happy Sailing!

Take a challenge

'Take a challenge and log your results'

At the end of each stage, and not part of the main course or certificate, are some fun things for you to try. Get your instructor to sign the book to say you have completed them!

Each 'Take a Challenge' is designed to improve your skills and techniques in all aspects of sailing by just being out on the water and having fun!

ONBOARD
RYA

It's time to get OnBoard!

OnBoard is the RYA's grass-roots programme for junior sailing and windsurfing. OnBoard is a safe, fun, and easily accessible way for anyone aged 8 to 18 who wants to get on the water and continue sailing through a structured and progressive programme.

You can start with just a taster, and then sail more regularly with OnBoard sessions, progressing through the RYA Stages as you go.

It's the perfect opportunity to make new friends, improve your mental and physical health and develop key life skills such as creativity, confidence, teamwork, determination, communication, and independence.

You don't need a boat and you don't need any fancy kit – you just need you to get OnBoard!

Creativity

Creativity involves having good ideas, dealing with uncertainty, and being able to make links between apparently unconnected things. Creative people have made great discoveries through seeing connections where others have not.

Confidence

Being confident involves being a can-do person, and being able to act independently. We gain more self-belief when we understand that making mistakes is normal, and know that the smart thing to do is to put in extra effort to work hard to improve.

Teamwork

Being a team player requires the ability to listen, show kindness to others, and give and receive feedback well. Giving helpful feedback is a difficult skill, but once learned it is very useful in many situations and an essential element of effective teamwork.

Communication

Communicating well is very important. A lot of unhappiness comes from accidental misunderstandings or careless explanations. Communication involves learning how to offer opinions. It also includes how to match language to the audience or person receiving the communication.

Determination

Determination involves coping with difficulty. When we get stuck, we need to have strategies for getting unstuck! Sometimes we also need to know how to bounce back after setbacks, rather than giving up.

Independence

Independence is not just about learning to do things yourself. It's also about knowing how to get the best out of those around you. Becoming independent is a fundamental part of growing up, and includes making decisions and dealing with responsibility.

Taking the next step and getting involved is easy. The OnBoard programme runs at over 280 RYA-approved OnBoard sailing and windsurfing clubs and centres throughout the UK, and is open to anyone aged 8–18. For more detailed information and to find your nearest OnBoard club or centre, visit www.rya.org.uk/start-boating/get-onboard-childrens-sailing, email us at onboard@rya.org.uk or call us on 02380 604 100.

Stage 1

During this course you will learn the basics of sailing, parts of the boat and how to launch, recover, and steer. After completing Stage 1, you will understand the basic principles of sailing in order to move on to Stage 2. No prior knowledge or experience of sailing is needed to take up this course.

Practical

Tick Here

Rigging
✓ Can assist with rigging a boat.

Launching & Recovery*
✓ Can launch a dinghy and get under way with instruction.
✓ Can secure boat to trolley.
✓ Can assist with recovery and stowage of dinghy and gear.

Ropework
✓ Can tie a figure of eight knot and cleat a halyard.

Sailing Techniques & Manoeuvres
Can be a responsive crew under instruction.**
✓ Can steer when sailing and being towed.
✓ Can steer on a reach and go about (reach to reach).
Understands the effect of basic boat controls.
✓ Understands the basic principles of stopping, controlling speed and getting out of irons.
✓ Can paddle or row (with sprit, paddle or oars).
✓ Can call for assistance.

Clothing & Equipment
✓ Can put on personal buoyancy correctly.
✓ Is confident in the water wearing personal buoyancy.

Capsize Recovery
Understands the importance of staying with the boat.*

Sailing Background

✓ Can name basic parts of a boat (i.e. hull, mast, rudder, tiller, centreboard, sheets etc.).
✓ Understands what action to take to assist those needing help.
✓ Understands how to prepare for a tow.

Clothing & Equipment
✓ Understands personal safety – and knows what to wear for sailing (including head and footwear).

Meteorology
✓ Has knowledge of wind direction.

Other Aspects and Options

- The Stage 2 course.
- Regular activity (clubs/OnBoard).

*Not keelboats
**Not singlehanders

ALL SECTIONS COMPLETED

_____
Instructor's signature

RYA

Youth Sailing Scheme

Stage 1

This is to certify that

Hugh

has completed all the requirements of this award to the standards laid down in the RYA Youth Sailing Scheme

Signed _____

Of _____

Principal/Chief Instructor

Date _1/8/2020_

Recognised Training Centre

Assistance required to complete the course ☐

106050

Please specify _____

Take the Next Step!

Learning to sail is great fun! Now you've learnt the basics, the next step is to improve your skills! Sailing is a fantastic sport with so much to do when you are on the water – you can sail with family and friends, learn to race or take an adventure by going on a journey. The choice is yours. So, don't stop here – the fun has only just begun! See you on the water!

What's Next?

▼

Stage 2

Want to find out more about where you can improve your skills with the next RYA course, or find your local training centre or club? Check out:

find.rya.org.uk

Call: 02380 604 100

E-mail: training@rya.org.uk

Please let us know how we did by giving us feedback at rya.org.uk/training/course-feedback

www.rya.org.uk

Take a Challenge

> Can you clap your hands while sailing?

> Why not challenge your friends to see who can rig the quickest?

> Starting from the beach as a group, sail or paddle out to a buoy and return to the shore. Perhaps even get into teams and make the challenge into a relay!

> By the end of this introductory course you will have a basic understanding of how a boat sails, and some experience of steering and handling the boat. Stages 2, 3 and 4 will complete your introduction to the sport in easy stages.

Stage 1

Stage 2

During this course you will continue to develop basic sailing skills, as well as ropework and collision avoidance. You will be able to tack and control boat speeds, leaving you in a good position to progress to Stage 3.

Tick Here

Practical

Rigging
✓ Can put a boat head to wind for rigging.
✓ Can rig a dinghy.

Launching & Recovery*
✓ Understands how to manoeuvre a trolley clear of other boats and overhead cables.
✓ Can launch and recover a small dinghy.

Ropework
✓ Can tie a round turn & two half hitches and a reef knot.

Sailing Techniques & Manoeuvres
Can control speed, and stop by lying-to.
Can get out of irons.
✓ Can go about (close reach to close reach).
Can crew a boat effectively.**
✓ Can sail a shallow triangle across the wind under supervision (gybing optional).

Understands the Principles of:
The five essentials.
✓ Returning to a beach* or pontoon.

Capsize Recovery*
Can be scooped in during capsize recovery**

or

✓ Can right one type of dinghy.

*Not keelboats
**Not singlehanders

Sailing Background

Sailing Manoeuvres
✓ Understands the No Go Zone.
Understands what is meant by windward, leeward and gybe.

General
Has knowledge of:
✓ Spars and rigging.
✓ Parts of the sail.
✓ Sail controls and foils.
✓ Offshore and onshore winds.
✓ Knows the importance of telling someone ashore you are going afloat.
✓ The dangers of human-made hazards, e.g. overhead power lines, weirs.

Rules of the Road
Has knowledge of port/starboard rule.

Meteorology
✓ Understands several ways of finding wind direction.

Clothing & Equipment
✓ Can choose and correctly adjust a personal buoyancy aid.
✓ Understands what to wear.

ALL SECTIONS COMPLETED

_____
Instructor's signature

Other Aspects and Options

- The Stage 3 course.
- Opportunities for regular practice.
- Club activity.

Take a Challenge

> _____ Get your instructor to write the parts of a boat on a card. Have a race with your group and see who can label them the quickest!

> _____ Can you drag one leg in the water while sailing along?

> _____ Ask your instructor to set up a race with a difference. At some marks you will score high being first, but at others you aim to be last! This will really test your boat control!

> _____ By the end of this course you will have a range of sailing skills and background knowledge, and be well on the way to being a confident small-boat sailor.

Stage 3

In Stage 3 you will continue to develop rigging and sailing techniques, capsize recovery and sailing theory, as well as launching and recovery skills. On completion of the course, you will be able to launch and sail a dinghy around a triangle in moderate conditions.

Practical

Rigging, Launching & Recovery*

> ✓____ Can rig, launch and recover in a variety of winds.

> ____ Can reef a dinghy ashore according to weather conditions.

> ____ Can store a dinghy ashore.

Ropework

> ____ Can tie a bowline, clove hitch and rolling hitch.

Sailing Techniques & Manoeuvres

Can demonstrate the basic principles of the following:

> ____ The five essentials.

> ____ Sail setting.

> ____ Balance.

> ____ Trim.

> ____ Sailing on all points of sail on a triangular course.

> ____ Tacking upwind.

> ____ Gybing from a training run.

> ____ Righting a small capsized dinghy as helm/crew.*

> ____ Coming alongside a moored boat.

> ____ Preparing for/taking up tow from power craft.

> ____ Picking up a mooring.

> ____ Understands how to and can recover a man overboard.

Racing

> ____ Understands the course and starting procedure.

*Not keelboats

Sailing Background

Manoeuvres

> ____ Understands the points of sailing.

General

> ____ Understands how a sail works – basic aerodynamics.

> ____ Knows basic terminology for use afloat (windward, leeward, bear away, luff up).

> ____ Understands the importance of clear communication aboard.

> ____ Understands lee-shore dangers and sailing in close company with other water users.

> ____ Understands advice to inland sailors for coastal sailing.

> ____ Knows the importance of personal safety and telling someone ashore.

> ____ Understands the dangers of hypothermia and the use of correct clothing for protection.

> ____ Understands the basic principles of Sail Safe: The 7 Common Senses (please see the inside back cover).

Rules of the Road

> ____ Knows the basic rules of the road – port/starboard, windward boat and overtaking boat.

ALL SECTIONS COMPLETED

_____

Instructor's signature

Meteorology

> _____ Knows how to obtain a weather forecast.

> _____ Understands Beaufort Wind Scale.

> _____ Knows when to reef.

Clothing & Equipment

Understands the importance of:

> _____ Personal safety equipment.

> _____ Boat buoyancy.

> _____ Basic safety equipment, e.g. anchor, paddle, bailer.

Other Aspects and Options

- The Stage 4 course.
- Regular practice and club activity.
- An introduction to the racing syllabus and the Start Racing course.
- RYA Foiling courses and opportunities.

Take a Challenge

> _____ Can you sail a triangular course with no centreboard?

> _____ Scatter balls in a sailing area set by your instructor and see who can collect the most out of your group of friends when returning them to your instructor's boat.

> _____ Ask your instructor to lay a box course. The aim is to see who can stay within the box the longest without being forced out by the other boats.

> _____ Having completed Stage 3 you will be able to sail in any direction and rig and launch your boat. Your skills and knowledge mean that you can regard yourself as a sailor, not a beginner.

Stage 4

Learn to sail a double-handed boat as crew or helm, applying all the skills you have learnt up to and including Stage 3, as well as gaining a variety of exciting new skills afloat.

Practical

Rigging & Launching

Can carry out the following tasks in all wind directions:

Tick Here

- ✓ Rig.
- _____ Launch.
- _____ Recover.
- _____ Can set up a boat according to weather conditions using sail and rig controls, e.g. mast rake, reefing.

Ropework

Knows the uses of and can tie:

- _____ Figure of eight.
- _____ Round turn & two half hitches.
- _____ Reef knot.
- _____ Bowline.
- _____ Clove hitch.
- _____ Rolling hitch.
- _____ Sheet bend.

Sailing Techniques & Manoeuvres

Can demonstrate:

- _____ Sailing techniques and manoeuvres from Stage 3 in a crewed boat.
- _____ Effective communication as helm and crew.
- _____ Effective use of the five essentials by helm and crew afloat including use of tell-tales.
- _____ Recovering a man overboard.
- _____ Righting a small capsized dinghy as helm/crew.*
- _____ Returning to a beach,* jetty or mooring safely in any wind direction.

*Not keelboats

Sailing Background

Has knowledge of:

- _____ IRPCS.
- _____ Beaufort Scale.
- _____ Synoptic charts.
- _____ Tidal ebb and flow.
- _____ Spring and neap tides.
- _____ How to recover from total inversion.*
- _____ Considerations for coastal sailing.
- _____ Applying the IRPCS afloat.
- _____ IALA buoyage, how to use tide tables and how to find the direction of tidal streams.

Other Aspects and Options

- _____ Advance your skills with one of the Advanced Modules.
- _____ RYA Racing Pathway options.
- _____ Regular practice and club activity.
- _____ Start your progression to becoming an Assistant Instructor and volunteering at your local club or centre.
- _____ RYA Foiling courses and opportunities.

ALL SECTIONS COMPLETED

_____

Instructor's signature

Take a Challenge

> See if you can learn to sail your boat backwards.

> Can you tie three knots blindfolded?

> Ask your instructor to lay a course setting a challenge to see how many tacks and gybes you can complete on the upwind and downwind legs.

> A Stage 4 certificate means that you have the skills to sail a double-handed boat as crew or helm, and solve a variety of problems afloat. Passing this course is the natural entry point for the advanced courses.

> Once you have learned to helm and crew a small boat, all sorts of opportunities in sailing are open to you...

Advanced Modules

As in all sports, practice is essential if you are to improve your skills and the best way to become a good sailor is to sail a variety of types of boats in different conditions.

Having practised your skills, one of the best ways to try a different type of sailing is to take another RYA course.

Following Stage 4, you have a choice of Advanced Modules in the RYA National Sailing Scheme. All of these can be run in two days, or an equivalent series of sessions over a longer period of time. Each course will introduce you to a different type of sailing, and may involve other classes of boat, depending on what is available locally.

Seamanship Skills

Seamanship Skills will help you learn skills a short step beyond Stage 4. During this course you will polish and test your skills and learn to resolve problems afloat. The course will give you a solid foundation for the future and enable you to become much more confident and self-sufficient afloat.

Tick Here

Practical

Ropework

> ✓ Can tie a fisherman's bend and sheet bend.

> _____ Can do heat sealing & whipping.

Launching & Recovery

Can leave and return to beach, jetty or mooring:

> _____ Windward shore.

> _____ Leeward shore.

Sailing Techniques & Manoeuvres

Is able to:

> _____ Heave to.

> _____ Reef afloat.

> _____ Recover MOB.

> _____ Be towed.

> _____ Anchor.†

> _____ Sail backwards.

> _____ Sail in adverse circumstances.*†

> _____ Knows how to prepare road trailer and secure ashore.

Coastal Option

> _____ Capable of practical application of skills in coastal waters.

> _____ Can use local tide tables.

> _____ Understands Rule of Twelfths and is aware of tidal streams.

> _____ Has a basic understanding of charts and important symbols.

Sailing Background

Sailing Theory

> _____ Understands terminology: windward, leeward, abeam, forward, aft, ahead, astern, to weather, downwind, amidships, quarter, pinching, sailing by the lee, luff, bear away, planing, sternway, broaching.

> _____ Knows and can apply Sail Safe: The 7 Common Senses (please see the inside front cover).

Knows and can apply the following International Regulations for Preventing Collisions at Sea (IRPCS):

> _____ Meeting other sailing vessels.

> _____ Meeting power-driven vessels.

> _____ Following or crossing narrow channels.

> _____ Action by stand-on vessel.

Capsize Recovery

> _____ Knows how to recover from total inversion.

ALL SECTIONS COMPLETED

_____

Instructor's signature

Seamanship Skills

Meteorology

> _____ Knows sources of information on weather patterns for day.

> _____ Can interpret forecasts and understand local effect.

> _____ Aware of Beaufort Scale and changing weather conditions.

Not necessarily applicable to keelboats
†Not necessarily applicable to multihulls*

Experienced Sailor's Direct Assessment

Sailors must satisfactorily complete the practical elements and answer questions on the theory sections. Candidates seeking assessment on coastal waters will demonstrate knowledge from the coastal section.

Sailing with Spinnakers

A very short but fun and thrilling syllabus which probably packs the most enjoyment of all the RYA courses. Everything you need to know to enjoy modern, three-sail boats.

Tick Here

Practical

Rigging

☑ _____ Can rig boats including spinnakers and trapeze where fitted.

Launching & Recovery

> _____ Understands how to launch boats with open transoms/racks.*†

Sailing Techniques & Manoeuvres

> _____ Sail as crew or helm using equipment to advantage.

Perform the following as helm or crew:

> _____ Hoist.

> _____ Gybe.

> _____ Drop.

> _____ Understands and can sail best course downwind.

Capsize Recovery

> _____ Perform capsize recovery with spinnaker.

> _____ Knows how to recover from inversion.*

Sailing Background

Racing

> _____ Has knowledge of courses for type of boat.

Sailing Theory & Background

> _____ Understands the concept of apparent wind.

> _____ Understands the effect of hull shapes on performance.

> _____ Sources of information and apply rig set-up for different conditions.

Not necessarily applicable to keelboats†Not necessarily applicable to multihulls

ALL SECTIONS COMPLETED

_____

Instructor's signature

Sailing with Spinnakers

Experienced Sailor's Direct Assessment

The candidate will complete all of the practical elements demonstrating a competent, purposeful and confident approach to an instructor. They will satisfactorily answer questions on the theory section afloat and ashore.

Day Sailing

If you sail at a coastal location you can explore the local sailing area, as well as developing your passage-planning and decision-making skills to go on a day sail or short journey. Basic pilotage and dealing with windy conditions are also covered.

Tick Here

Practical

Rigging

> ✓ Can prepare and equip a boat for a day sail or short journey including safety and navigation equipment, clothing, and food.

> ____ Can stow gear correctly.

Sailing Techniques & Manoeuvres

> ____ Can plan and undertake a day sail including a consideration of pilotage/navigation and collision avoidance.

> ____ Can use anchor to effect lee shore landing and departure.*†

> ____ Adverse conditions.

> ____ Is able to self-rescue following total inversion.*

> ____ Understands how to improvise in the event of gear failure.

Sailing Background

Sailing Theory & Background

> ____ Has knowledge of boat handling in strong winds and difficult conditions (practical where possible).

Navigation

Can plan a day sail or short journey in coastal waters, including knowledge of:

> ____ Publications, i.e. charts, tide tables.

> ____ Navigation instruments.

> ____ Use of GPS.

> ____ Tidal heights and streams.

> ____ Rule of Twelfths.

> ____ Decision making including planning alternatives.

> ____ Magnetic compass: variation/deviation.

> ____ Chart work.

> ____ Use of transits and bearings to steer and position fix.

> ____ Recording position and dead reckoning.

ALL SECTIONS COMPLETED

_____

Instructor's signature

Meteorology

> _____ Knows sources of information on weather patterns.
> _____ Understands high- and low-pressure systems.

Has awareness of:

> _____ Changing weather conditions.
> _____ Understands simple synoptic charts.

*Not necessarily applicable to keelboats
†Not necessarily applicable to multihulls

Experienced Sailor's Direct Assessment

Sailors will complete all of the practical elements demonstrating a competent, purposeful and safe approach, and will also be asked to answer questions on the theoretical sections and whenever possible demonstrate skills satisfactorily afloat and ashore.

Performance Sailing

Improve your boat handling and confidence in performance boats. This is an opportunity to be coached, practise your helming and crewing and work on a smooth, fluent sailing performance with or without the spinnaker.

Tick Here

Practical

Rigging

> ✓____ Can rig any type of boat, including spinnaker and trapeze (if equipped).

Sailing Techniques & Manoeuvres

> ____ Can make best possible use of crew and equipment to sail efficiently on all points of sailing in a variety of conditions, including symmetric or asymmetric spinnakers (where possible).

> ____ Can spot and use wind shifts and gusts to effect best course up/downwind.

> ____ Can perform capsize recovery with spinnaker.*

> ____ Knows how to recover from total inversion.

Sailing Background

Sailing Theory

> ____ Understands how to make use of wind variations and tidal eddies.

> ____ Has an understanding of hull shape and rig types including their effect on performance.

> ____ Understands planing and effect of rails.

Meteorology

> ____ Knows sources of information on weather patterns for the day.

> ____ Understands main characteristics of high- and low-pressure systems and simple interpretation of synoptic charts.

> ____ Has awareness of changing weather conditions.

Not applicable to keelboats

ALL SECTIONS COMPLETED

_____

Instructor's signature

Experienced Sailor's Direct Assessment

Sailors must complete all of the practical elements demonstrating a competent, purposeful and safe approach to sailing performance boats, and must also answer questions on the theoretical sections and whenever possible demonstrate skills satisfactorily afloat and ashore.

First Flights Foiling

This first session in sail-foiling provides an initial introduction into the amazing and exhilarating world of foiling. Every student starting this course should have completed Stage 4 of the RYA Youth Sailing Scheme, which will ensure you have the necessary skills to take on foiling! Aimed as a taster session, First Flights provides you with a basic introduction to foiling, assisting you to make your first foiling take-offs.

Practical

Tick Here

Rigging

Has knowledge of:

> ___ Assembling and setting up the main foil, rudder, and rudder foil.

> ___ Various foiling boats.

> ___ The options and adaptions available for non-foiling boats.

Launching and recovery:

> ___ Has knowledge of the different launch/recovery methods for different boat designs.

Sailing Techniques & Manoeuvres

Can:

> ___ Engage and disengage foils.

> ___ Change course sailed, and adjust sail trim to encourage flight.

> ___ Take off.

Understands and has knowledge of:

> ___ How to land safely.

> ___ How to maintain foiling.

> ___ Capsize-recovery methods.

> ___ Apparent wind, showing a basic application and sail adjustment.

Foiling Knowledge

Understands and has knowledge of:

> ___ The basic theory of how foils work.

> ___ A range of different foiling boats.

> ___ Sail adjustments, and how to trim sails.

Safety

Understands and has knowledge of:

> ___ The risks of foiling alone.

> ___ The lack of noise when approaching other craft.

> ___ Different personal safety equipment.

> ___ The importance of foiling in suitable sailing conditions.

ALL SECTIONS COMPLETED

_____

Instructor's signature

First Flights Foiling

Start Racing

The first course in the racing syllabus, Start Racing, will develop and provide you with the basic skills needed to enter a race and understand the simple techniques, sequences, and rules. To take this course every student should have mastered the practical skills to Level 2/Stage 3 or above.

Starts

> ✓ Understands a basic start sequence.

> _____ Can identify a start line and start from the correct side.

> _____ Can slow the boat and accelerate to cross the line within 10 seconds after the start signal.

> _____ Understands the procedure if over the line at the start.

> _____ Understands the significance of port/starboard and windward/leeward.

Boat Handling

> _____ Can tack and gybe in a range of conditions.

> _____ Understands the use of heel and trim to aid steering.

> _____ Understands an appropriate technique to approach and land when coming ashore, on lee shores, weather shores, or slipways.

> _____ Can recover from a capsize with little assistance.

> _____ Can perform an MOB recovery to Level 2 standard.

Speed

> _____ Can use the five essentials effectively.

> _____ Can keep the boat upright using the toe straps to sit out and can trim the sail to aid this.

> _____ Can hold an effective close-hauled course upwind.

Tactics

> _____ Understands how to round a mark.

> _____ Can recognise headers and lifts.

> _____ Has knowledge of the difference between the International Regulations for Preventing Collisions at Sea (IRPCS) and the Racing Rules of Sailing (RRS). Understands other rules as shown.

Strategy

> _____ Can source and use an appropriate weather forecast.

> _____ Understands what a suitable wind strength is to race in.

ALL SECTIONS COMPLETED

_____

Instructor's/Racing Coach's signature

Take a Challenge

> _____ Take part in a club race.

What are the following terms, or what do they stand for?

> _____ a. Being in irons.

> _____ b. The five essentials.

> _____ c. To 'luff up'.

> _____ d. Beaufort Scale.

> _____ e. Racing Rules of Sailing (RRS).

Club Racing

The Club Racing course has been designed to improve boat handling and speed, whilst providing an understanding of developing a strategic plan based on the conditions. Students taking this course should have the minimum knowledge of Start Racing.

Tick Here

Starts

> ✓ Understands line bias and can identify the biased end.

> ____ Has knowledge of how the fleet of boats may impact on the start strategy.

> ____ Understands how the strategy for the first beat may impact the starting position.

> ____ Can successfully start on their home club line (for sailors completing the course at their home-club).

Boat Handling

> ____ Can slow the boat effectively and accelerate.

> ____ Can use heel to help the boat tack and gybe.

> ____ If appropriate, can hoist, gybe, fly, and drop a spinnaker.

> ____ Can demonstrate the importance of good communication and teamwork for effective racing.

Speed

> ____ Can adapt the rig to different conditions.

> ____ Can use a tuning guide appropriate to the boat being used.

Tactics

> ____ Understands the significance of laylines and how to judge them when afloat.

> ____ Understands the importance of clean air.

> ____ Understands tactics within a handicap fleet (if appropriate).

> ____ Can demonstrate application of Section A and Section B of the Racing Rules of Sailing (RRS).

> ____ Understands how the rules apply at marks and obstructions (Section C of the RRS).

Strategy

> ____ Understands the effect of water current on the boat and how the topography (buildings, trees, hills) can affect the wind over a course.

> ____ Can use a suitable weather app to give an indication of wind trend over the period of a race and how to use that to best effect.

> ____ Can occasionally demonstrate the ability to tack or gybe on wind shifts.

ALL SECTIONS COMPLETED

_____

Instructor's/Racing Coach's signature

Other Aspects

- Has knowledge of, and participates regularly in club racing.

Take a Challenge

> _____ Attend club race training.

> _____ Try a pursuit race.

> _____ Try a handicap race.

Regional Racing

Learn and develop skills which will enhance your ability to adapt to the changing conditions and different venues, as well as the skills needed to respond. Regional Racing will also provide the skills and techniques needed to analyse effectively post-race.

Starts

- ✓_____ Can create and protect a space to leeward.
- _____ Can demonstrate starting from different parts of the start line.
- _____ Can formulate and execute a pre-start plan.
- _____ Can demonstrate a practical understanding of the signals explained in Part 3 of the Racing Rules of Sailing (RRS).

Boat Handling

- _____ Can adapt to different types of boat.
- _____ Understands the different techniques used for a range of different craft.
- _____ Can demonstrate all previous learning over a wide range of wind conditions where possible.

Speed

- _____ Understands the differences between stayed rigs and unstayed rigs.
- _____ Can alter the rig while racing to suit conditions where possible.
- _____ Understands how to record settings and duplicate them.

Tactics

- _____ Can identify the layline for a mark and allow for the conditions and the effect of the fleet.
- _____ Understands the importance of when to sail the fleet and when to engage with another boat.
- _____ Can demonstrate both a tight and loose cover on another boat.
- _____ Has knowledge of how to use a compass to best effect.
- _____ Understands all of Part 2 of the Racing Rules of Sailing (RRS) and can demonstrate taking a penalty effectively.
- _____ Understands the process for raising a protest and actions when being protested.

Strategy

- _____ Can develop a strategy that accounts for the weather conditions expected, the tide/current expected, and the type of fleet. This should be discussed with the coach/instructor prior to the race and will be seen to be executed.

ALL SECTIONS COMPLETED

_____

Instructor's/Racing Coach's signature

Regional Racing

Take a Challenge

Attend:

- _____ An open meeting.
- _____ Class open training.
- _____ RYA regional training.
- _____ Regional Junior Championships.

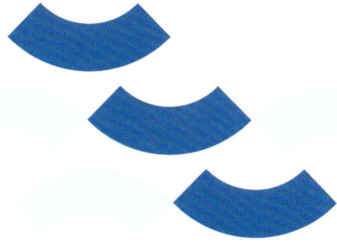

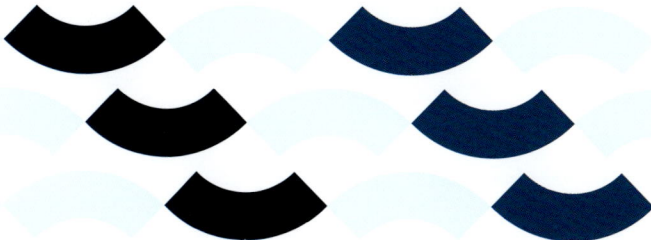

Championship Racing

This is more personalised training than a course, and requires a less syllabus-based approach, taking into consideration the needs of the sailor and varying the areas covered accordingly. It is quite likely to be the end result of a full training programme. Championship Racing is run by an RYA Race Coach Level 3, over a minimum of 50 hours.

Tick Here

Starts

> ✓____ Can take the strategy and adopt the most applicable start.

> ____ Can recover and adapt the start where appropriate.

> ____ Can demonstrate recovering from a start which has not gone to plan.

Boat Handling

> ____ Can demonstrate a high level of boat handling in all conditions and is able to adapt the techniques used to suit conditions.

> ____ Can use analysis to develop improved techniques.

Speed

> ____ Understands how to keep records of the settings and to develop them to suit the conditions/sailors.

> ____ Understands how to use a tuning partner, video, and post-race analysis to refine further the tuning guide and techniques employed.

> ____ Can develop and demonstrate how to sail in different conditions.

Tactics

> ____ Understands all the relevant racing rules and how to use them to best effect for the outcome of the race.

> ____ Understands how to analyse a series of races and to implement strategies to secure the best outcome.

> ____ Understands when to race conservatively and when to race aggressively and can demonstrate these.

> ____ Can demonstrate use of 'boat-on-boat' and 'boat-on-fleet' tactics during racing/training.

Strategy

> ____ Can develop, plan, and adapt the strategy to take into account the unfolding landscape of a race while still showing consistent boat speed.

ALL SECTIONS COMPLETED

_____

Instructor's/Racing Coach's signature

Championship Racing

Other Aspects

Participates regularly in:

• Open meetings.

• National class events.

• RYA Youth/Junior championships.

What's next?

Once you have completed Stage 4, the natural progression is to the Advanced Modules, or perhaps the Racing levels if you have completed Stage 3. However, here are some other areas of the sport that might be of interest.

Getting on the Water Regularly

Once you have completed some of the stages in this logbook, you might like to look for ways to get on the water regularly. Often the centre you have been going to will be able to talk you through the opportunities with them or locally. But with over 1,400 sailing clubs across the UK, inland and coastal, there is bound to be somewhere close by.

When you learn to sail, the RYA training centre or club will provide boats, but when you are looking to develop your skills you could sail with someone else, or buy your own boat. Sailing with an experienced person is a really good way to learn and many clubs run schemes to introduce new sailors into the club.

If you do decide to buy a boat the best way to select one is to find out what classes are sailed at your local club and which boat is best for your size and ability.

To find your nearest club or training centres, visit the RYA website: www.rya.org.uk/wheres-my-nearest

Becoming an Instructor and the Instructor Pathway

With sailing having grabbed your attention, you may wish to pass the skills you have learnt from this exhilarating sport on to others. Once you have gained one of the Advanced Modules, you can start your progression on the instructional ladder as an Assistant Instructor. On turning 16, you may choose to progress this and become a fully qualified RYA Dinghy Instructor.

If you have basic racing experience, you may enjoy the opportunity to learn basic race-coaching techniques. The Racing Instructor course covers instructional techniques ashore and afloat, allowing you to assist others to start their pathway to racing!

> Further details of the RYA National Sailing Scheme are available in RYA publication G4, the RYA National Sailing Scheme Syllabus & Logbook.

The Duke of Edinburgh's Award

Are you aged between 14 to 24 and fancy challenging yourself?

The RYA is recognised as a National Operating Authority for The Duke of Edinburgh's Award (DofE). The DofE is a voluntary, non-competitive programme of activities for anyone aged 14 to 24, providing a fantastic opportunity to experience new activities or develop existing skills.

There are three progressive levels of programmes that, when successfully completed, lead to a Bronze, Silver or Gold Award.

Sailing as part of your DofE

Achieving a DofE Award can be made an adventure from beginning to end. Within an RYA club or training centre there are already many activities you could take part in that can count towards your DofE. These could range from:

- Volunteering: Helping out at your local training centre, club or Team15 night on a regular basis. This could be as an assistant, in the kitchen or maybe even on the committee!

- Physical: Regularly taking part in sailing or windsurfing activity? Why not set yourself a goal to gain a certain certificate in the RYA National Sailing or Windsurfing scheme, or maybe participate in regular club racing?

- Skill: All about developing your skills, whether practical, social or personal. You may choose to sharpen up your powerboating, learn a new skill such as boat repair work, become an instructor or perhaps increase your theory knowledge and learn all about meteorology!

- Residential and Expedition: You may never have been away from home before, let alone used your board or boat to go on an exciting adventure with friends, so now is the time!

> Further information can be found, explaining the opportunities available, on the DofE website www.dofe.org, and the RYA website www.rya.org.uk/training/under-16s/the-duke-of-edinburgh-award

Get Into Racing

Racing is an exciting and sociable way to develop your sailing. Starting out can be a little daunting, so hopefully this information highlights the key areas you need to consider in learning to race, and gives guidance to help make your racing fun and rewarding.

There are a number of ways to go racing:

Sailing Clubs

Most racing in the UK is run by clubs, during the evening or weekends. Often clubs have a youth section and many run introduction to racing training sessions.

As a club member you may be able to hire a boat, or sail with another member, but in many clubs you need to have use of your own boat. Lots of clubs run regular courses and training to help sailors to improve at all levels. They may also host 'open meetings' for a particular class of boat (see below).

Clubs that run youth coaching are often granted British Youth Sailing (BYS) Recognised Club status. This means that they have a good-quality, safe and effective race-training programme that enthuses and develops young sailors. These clubs have strong links to the RYA Junior and Youth Pathway.

Choosing the right club will be an individual decision but here are some questions to consider:

- Do they run training for novice sailors?
- Is the sailing area safe for novices?
- What classes of dinghy do they race and when?
- How much is membership and what does it include?
- Do I need to buy a boat?

Class Associations

Members of these organisations sail the same class of boat. There will be an active programme of open meetings and often accessible class training that is run regionally. The class association will frequently run national racing events, which less experienced sailors may aspire to attend as they progress. Most class members have a home sailing club, but may also travel to attend open meetings.

RYA Training Groups

The RYA runs Regional Training Groups (RTGs) in all the regions in England. The home countries have their own programmes including open training and squads. These help to develop young racers across the junior age groups. RYA training is in the following classes:

RTGs and Home Country Squads – (normally under 14/15)

Optimist, Topper, RS Feva XL, ILCA 4, Bic Techno 293OD (Windsurfer)

RS Tera and Cadet classes are RYA Recognised Classes who run their own training and competitions.

Youth Performance Squads – (normally under 19)

Youth sailing typically takes place from around 15 years of age. The class associations run open training supported by the RYA for their less-experienced sailors. The more-experienced sailors are selected for the Youth Performance Squads.

The following are RYA Recognised Classes:

ILCA 6, ILCA 7, 420, 29er, iQFOiL, Nacra 15, Kites

Each squad has specific training programmes and selection criteria. Further details may be found in the 'Racing' section of the RYA website or via the RYA Racing Department.

These Junior and Youth Programmes are underpinned by the BYS Recognised Club Programme and together form the national pathway for developing and supporting talented young racers. Further information may also be found in the RYA Youth Racing Programme Handbook, available from the RYA Racing Department or your local Regional Performance Manager.

E-mail: youthracing@rya.org.uk

BRITISH YOUTH SAILING RYA

Personal Log

Date	Class of boat	Hours' experience		Activity and weather conditions		Centre/club
		Helm	Crew	Type of course or activity	Max wind speed	Instructor/ coach

Date	Class of boat	Hours' experience		Activity and weather conditions		Centre/club
		Helm	Crew	Type of course or activity	Max wind speed	Instructor/ coach

Personal Log

Date	Class of boat	Hours' experience		Activity and weather conditions		Centre/club
		Helm	Crew	Type of course or activity	Max wind speed	Instructor/ coach

Personal Log

Date	Class of boat	Hours' experience		Activity and weather conditions		Centre/club
		Helm	Crew	Type of course or activity	Max wind speed	Instructor/ coach

Course Certificates

Stage 1

Course Certificates

Stage 2

Course Certificates

Stage 3

Stage 4

Course Certificates

Seamanship Skills

Sailing with Spinnakers

Course Certificates

Day Sailing

Course Certificates

Performance Sailing

Course Certificates

First Flights Foiling

Course Certificates

Start Racing

Course Certificates

Club Racing

Regional Racing

Course Certificates

Championship Racing